Catherine

by

Josephine Mattia

Acknowledgement

First and Foremost, I thank God, Blessed Mother Mary, Saints Joseph, Bernadette & Bakhita and the Divino Nino for giving me a wonderful, spiritual guidance in working and presenting these Poems & Haikus.

My Family: My Mom Mary Mattia, Siblings Stephen & Stephanie and My Niece & Nephew, Jude & Keva. Your prayers and support mean so much to me. Thanks for all the love and positivity.

My Professors David Bottoms and Dr. Simona Weik for your guidance and support throughout my journey as a Poet.

I also dedicate this Chapbook to my Niece, Luna Elisha Mattia.

Table of Contents

Magnolia

I stroll through the Park,

dozens of Magnolias bloom in

the trees,

lovely like the morning sun, young

like a fresh Sakura. I see people

everywhere taking photos

of these flowers due to their radiance and beauty.

I continue my walk when a young man gives

me a bunch of Magnolias, and places

them in my hand. "For you, my Magnolia," he says,

and quietly goes along on his stroll. Speechless,

I carry the Magnolias until I come home.

I reach my destination, as I sit in the front steps

of my home, pulling out one of the Magnolias. I

look at each leaf, plucking them out one by one.

Suddenly, the wind blows hard in my direction,

and all the Magnolias are blown away. I look up

In the sky, and they are placing themselves in the

arms of the angels in Heaven.

Girl at a Party

The scene of kids dancing to the sounds of

The Coasters' music in the Basement of my home,

I see a girl standing outside the edge of the dance

floor, dressed in White with hair neatly combed

and creepers, in contrast to the Saddle Shoes, Leather

Jackets, Denim Jeans, Beehives and Ducktails. She

walks through the crowd, praying that someone will

dance with her. The music changes from The Coasters

to The Four Aces through the speakers; everyone

partners up, knowing she missed her chance to speak.

Couples dance closer, staring at each other's faces

while the Girl smiles, excluding insecurity and says to

herself, "It will be all right." Silently, she removes herself

from the floor to the chair, with a couple of girls gossiping

about her nonconformist attitude. Her upbeat attitude

continues on throughout the night, eating merrily, dancing

by herself without a care to Gary U.S. Bonds, all while

onlookers shut their mouths. The Party ends, I say my

goodbyes to all of my guests. I finally get a chance to sit

down, watching the girl going up the stairs. The Basement

reeks of silence, still fixated on the lovely girl's presence

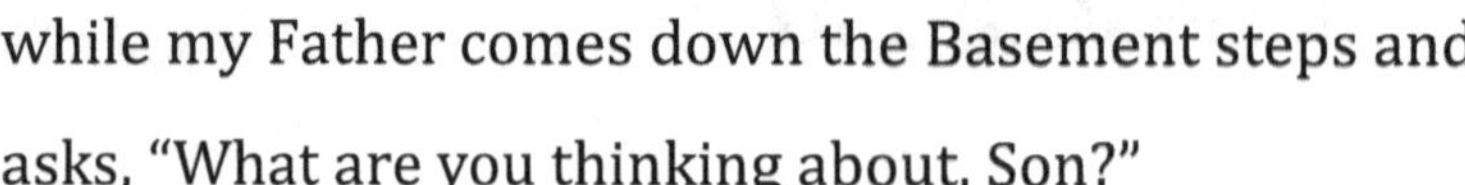

while my Father comes down the Basement steps and

asks, "What are you thinking about, Son?"

The Sixties

December 30th, 1969:

As I sit in the corner of my Bedroom,

flashes of numerous events rush in.

In 1960, a young, fresh leader told the

nation to explore "New Frontiers."

That was what he did, until three years later,

he died in his prime. Not a dry eye once Cronkite announced

it. A few days later, I witnessed a little boy giving a salute

to his Father, as they carried the casket.

A few months later, four young men with British

accents on television brought a sense of joy

after the madness, & everyone was on their feet

dancing their worries away. Along with these musical

icons, I witnessed a young married woman in 1965, sitting

on the steps of her home, crying because her husband

is heading off to Vietnam. "What will I do? What will I do?",

she cries not certain if he will come back dead or alive.

Three years later, radicalism is in and conservatism is out

as young people move out from middle America to Haight-Ashbury,

as their new home where lives are wasted away on the words

of Dr. Leary saying, "Turn On, Tune In, Drop Dead." I wept

along with the nation at home, when two of my heroes were

assassinated in Memphis & the Ambassador Hotel, respectively.

"Why must your children die for something that you have

instructed them to do?" I said to God. An unknown music

festival set the tone for the Hippie Generation, that the

world took notice, complete with a wonderful performance from

a troubled musician. "Play Jimi Play," the people say. Memories

of me and my family watching a man in a white spacesuit taking the

first step on the Moon, all while busy worrying if The Raiders will

perform on "The Ed Sullivan Show." All of these memories

of such an important decade makes me question,

"I wonder what will the next decade bring?"

Road to Confession

I

Will I make a sincere confession?

I asked myself, as I drove to Church.

The past mistakes, unchristian choices

and insensitivity rage

in my mind. I ignore my conscience,

as I make a STOP on South Hairston

Road. It is hard to control myself,

knowing when I lose my inhibitions, I

went crazy, running wild and free.

The Traffic Sign changes to green,

I moved on, continuing to reflect where

I stand morally. Besides, I fear what will

happen to me spiritually, in the future.

II

Is it too late for me to change?

Heavenly Father, I have let you down far

too many times when I knew I should be

following you. It is comprehensible, that

as an unmarried woman, my focus should

be on God. Facing a MERGE sign, once coming

up Redan Road, having a solemn look on my

face. When one is following a moral path, she

must be obedient, no matter the situation. Sadly,

missteps blocked my way for getting closer to God.

How could I correct the wrongdoings in my life?

III

I finally reach St. Alexander Catholic Church;

driving through the gates until I find a parking

spot, where I step out of the car. The sounds

of the Choir making heavenly music soothes

my soul as I enter the Church, sitting until

the Priest allows me to enter the confessional.

Haikus

Flower Petals

Petals in the water

Separate as each of them

Go their different ways.

Lilies in the Field

Lilies in the field

Blooming and blossoming

in the grass, one by one.

Here I Am

Here I am, standing

in the shadows; everything

in complete darkness.

The White Dress

There was a White Dress that I once owned.
Pure, like a Lily, beautiful like an evening
gown. The countless times wearing the dress
outdoors, letting it twirl as I roamed around
the fields like a little girl, barefoot, remembering
the time I got my first kiss in it. So innocent and
memorable, I made a weird sound on the way
home. Raindrops letting it soak while walking
in the rain, people think I married it. The
Dress is no longer there, as it became old
and worn. Other dresses come and go,
but the White Dress will always be in the
back of my mind.

October 15, 1958

Across the street,

I see a group of kids happily eating

Ice Cream outside of Debbie's Ice Cream

on Garner Avenue. I wait for the Bus,

wondering when I'll ever get the chance to

eat alongside my white brothers and sisters

knowing that society has divided us by race.

The Bus arrives, I get in paying for my fare.

"Blacks in the back, Ma'am," the Driver tells me;

the flash of redness spreads all over my face as the

seats up front are mostly empty. "Well, are you going

to sit down, or not?", says the Driver impatiently. "Yes Sir,"

I said in a polite manner. At the first stop, a couple

leaves, and I sit down gazing at the window.

Through the scenery, I see the unexpected.

Down the road, I see children from different races,

holding hands and playing with each other. No hate,

no quarreling, just peace and harmony.

I looked back and smiled. "Last stop, Ma'am," the Driver

says to me. I step out of the Bus, only this time

the children aren't there. All of this is a dream.

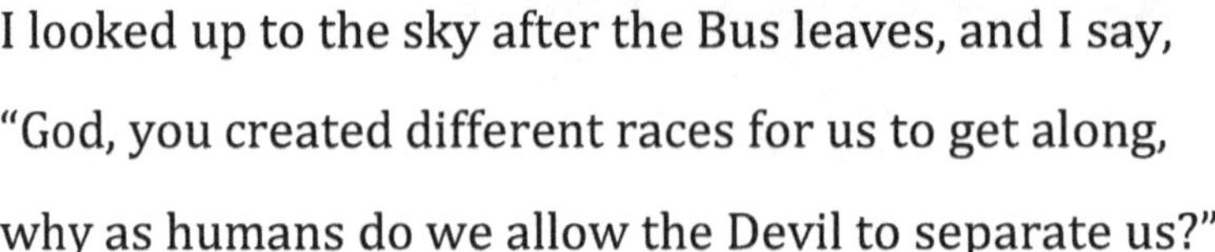

I looked up to the sky after the Bus leaves, and I say,

"God, you created different races for us to get along,

why as humans do we allow the Devil to separate us?"

Do You?

Do you dare? Do you dream?

Do you allow your dreams to come

True, or does it stay deferred?

Do you stay tempestuous,

Or do you remain calm like a Dove?

Do you act prim and proper, or do

You act reckless and nonchalant?

Do you live a clean, righteous life

Or do you a life of constant problems?

Do you prefer to live uptown where

You can live comfortably, or do you

Remain to stay Downtown where all

The eccentric characters and places

You call home?

Do you love to live life to the fullest

Or do you get hung up in the past?

Do you love to go out and explore,

Or do you prefer to stay indoors where

It's nice and quiet?

Please tell me, what kind of person

are you?

I am From

I am from where being a girly-girl rules,

but you will find me doing Embroidery

while sitting barefoot on the roof.

My spirit lies within the Catholic Faith,

therefore, I sing to the Divino Nino.

I am from an era where non-conformity rules:

belittling morality, even though old-school

is the way to go.

I am living in a one-room Motel, with a

Mother, two siblings, a Niece and Nephew

dreaming of a better life beyond the rowdy

environment smack dab in the middle of

the suburbs.

I am from listening to the sounds of

Ricky Nelson and Ellie Greenwich

blasting through the speakers of my

stereo, where I write three-line poetry.

The Language of a Poet

I have wanted to excel in the Poetry world,

I have wanted my works to have an impact

and be everlasting with perfect imagery,

language so I speak, it flows past my mouth

and the mind of readers.

I have wanted to use metaphors, give my

poems a chance to express in ways ordinary

language won't. I have tried to avoid clichés,

it's the only way for me to stop creating lazy poetry.

I have wanted bravery, I have imagined myself

not holding back, giving a proper "don't care,"

to anyone who has read my works. Forget the

consequences, I am no longer who I was previously;

all silence, no words.

My confidence builds once I walk to the theatre stage,

my nerves are no longer here,

my calm demeanor remains intact.

I finally have the chance to say my poem,

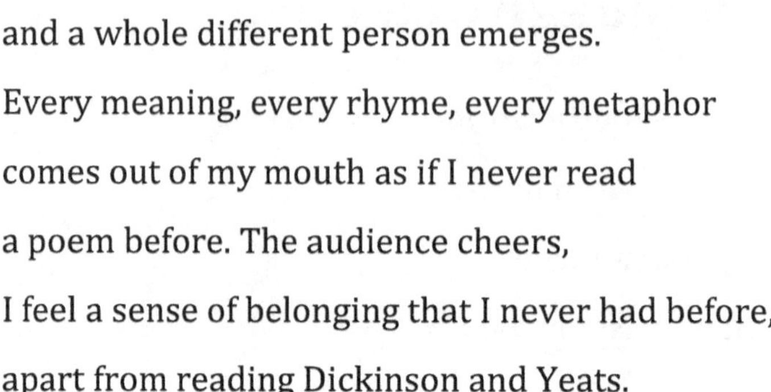

and a whole different person emerges.

Every meaning, every rhyme, every metaphor

comes out of my mouth as if I never read

a poem before. The audience cheers,

I feel a sense of belonging that I never had before,

apart from reading Dickinson and Yeats.

Oh, how I am free just like they are.

A Night Ride Home

Another Saturday night, and everyone is leaving

The house. The Party is officially over, food is

Scattered on tables, people carrying Balloons &

Babyface's "My Kinda Girl" is playing in the background.

Cars are pulling up the driveway amidst a sea of people

Surrounding me. I do the exact opposite by taking the

Long walk home. As I reach around the corner of

Windward Street, a Person driving a Light Blue 1958

Chevrolet convertible drives up closely to where I am walking.

The window Rolls down, and it is a classmate whom I knew well

With sandy Blonde hair, brown eyes, a smile that's impossible not to

Ignore and a cool demeanor. "Hello," he says in a calm, effortless

Manner. "You need a ride home?" Nodding me head yes, I

Sat in the front seat. "4521 Arbor Lane please," explaining where

My destination is located. We sat in silence on the way home, the

Only sound hearing The Imperials singing "Well, I'm think I'm

Going out of my head/over you…" Awkward looks were giving

Towards me a couple of times, not knowing what it meant.

Once he reaches my destination, we exchange our goodbyes.

Suddenly, the unexpected happened. He reaches for my left

Cheek and kisses it. Red in the face, I quickly exit his car.

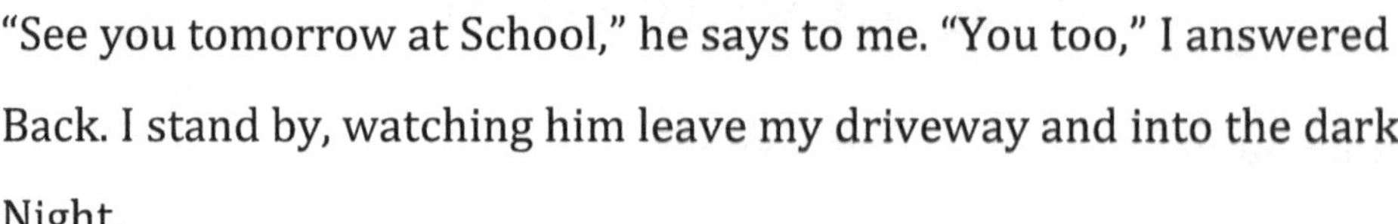

"See you tomorrow at School," he says to me. "You too," I answered Back. I stand by, watching him leave my driveway and into the dark Night.

The End